Index: 6 Beautiful Quilts Pieced with

Batik Beauty
pages 4 - 5 and 10 - 11

Love Fills Our Home
pages 8 - 9 and 15 - 17

Basket with Flowers
pages 6 - 7 and 12 - 14

Fuchsia
pages 32 - 33 and 24 - 25

Sugar and Spice
pages 34 - 35 and 26 - 29

Hydrangea
pages 30 - 31 and 22 - 23

Batik Beauty

pieced by Lanelle Herron
quilted by Susan Corbett

From the sundrenched glow of summer citrus to the purple haze of a twilight sky, batik quilts invigorate the senses with flowing color and light. The rich tones are simultaneously exciting and serene.

instructions on pages 10 - 11

Batik Colors

SIZE: 42" x 55"
MATERIALS:
   E. E. Schenck Company/Galaxy
   Java Batiks
Purchase 1 'Sweet 16s' pack OR 29 fabrics 9" x 11"

4 Dark Navy to Purple	or ¼ yd
3 Lavender/Pink	or ¼ yd
3 Yellow to Lime	or ¼ yd
5 Burgundy to Red	or ½ yd
5 Brown to Gold	or ½ yd
3 Orange to Yellow	or ¼ yd
4 Green to Olive	or ¼ yd
2 Turquoise to Blue	or ¼ yd

Inner Border	Purchase ¼ yd Purple
Binding	Purchase ½ yd Aqua
Backing	Purchase 1½ yds
Batting	Purchase 48" x 59"

Sewing machine, needles, thread

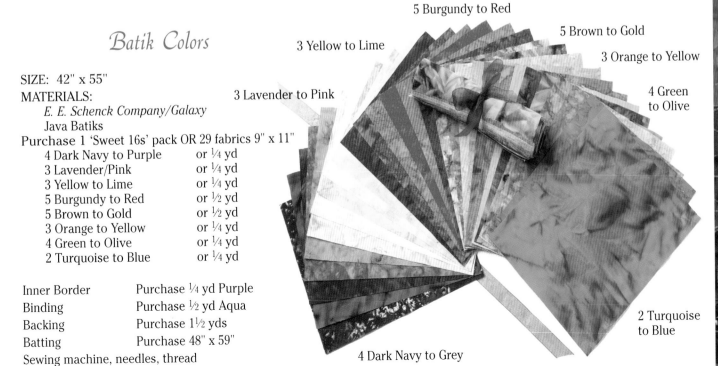

5 Burgundy to Red

3 Yellow to Lime

5 Brown to Gold

3 Orange to Yellow

3 Lavender to Pink

4 Green to Olive

2 Turquoise to Blue

4 Dark Navy to Grey

WillowBerry Basket of Flowers

pieced by Donna Perrotta
quilted by Susan Corbett

Beautiful borders outline this quilt with soft colors and enticing flowers.

Experience the joy of creating your own Broderie Perse applique on a small scale with flowers and a basket in the center of this stunning quilt.

instructions on pages 12 - 14

'Broderie Perse' Applique

The first "chintz", or painted cotton fabric, was imported to England from India in 1600. Eager to please the voracious demand of the western market, manufacturers chose floral designs and patterns from English art as well as popular Asian motifs.

Feeling a threat to the English wool and silk trade, the manufacture of chintz was banned in England and its colonies, which caused a limited supply and sky-rocketing prices. In response, women resorted to cutting out the motifs and sewing them to less costly background fabrics.

Broderie Perse is French for Persian embroidery and came to refer to the exquisite appliqué of printed chintz onto solid, usually whole-cloth, quilts.

These intricate quilts were originally made out of necessity, but since the 1700's, Broderie Perse has become a popular art on its own.

WillowBerry Winter Colors

SIZE: 47" x 47"

MATERIALS:

E. E. Schenck Company/Maywood Studio
WillowBerry Winter by WillowBerry Lane
Purchase 1 'Sweet 16s' pack OR 18 fabrics 9" x 11":

5 Peach prints	or ½ yd
6 Green prints	or ½ yd
5 Ivory/Tan prints	or ½ yd
1 Ivory/Peach stripe	or ¼ yd
1 Red check	or ¼ yd

Border & Binding	Purchase 2¾ yds Peach border print
Backing	Purchase 2 yds
Batting	Purchase 52" x 52"

Sewing machine, needle, thread

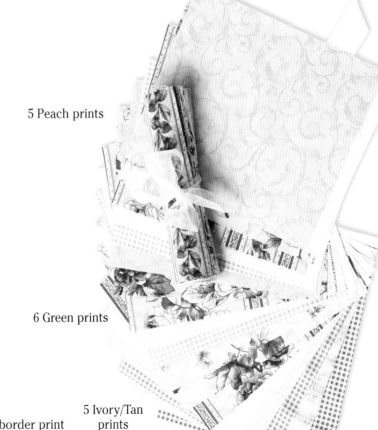

5 Peach prints

6 Green prints

5 Ivory/Tan prints

1 Ivory/Peach stripe

1 Red check

Love Fills Our Home

pieced by Donna Perrotta
quilted by Susan Corbett

Fill your home with sweet sentiments and soothing pastel colors. Love Fills Our Home presents an opportunity to exhibit a fabulous array of techniques all in one small project. Enjoy your appliqué and embroidery skills as well as your piecing expertise with this great six-border design.

instructions on pages 15 - 17

9 Peach prints, Light to Dark

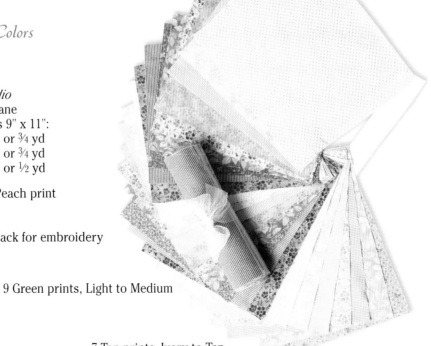

WillowBerry Basics Colors

SIZE: 41" x 47"

MATERIALS:
  E. E. Schenck Company/Maywood Studio
  WillowBerry Basics by WillowBerry Lane
  Purchase 1 'Sweet 16s' pack OR 25 fabrics 9" x 11":
    9 Peach prints, Light to Dark   or ¾ yd
    9 Green prints, Light to Medium   or ¾ yd
    7 Tan prints, Ivory to Tan   or ½ yd

Border & Binding   Purchase 1½ yds Peach print
Backing   Purchase 1¾ yds
Batting   Purchase 45" x 51"
Purchase *DMC* pearl cotton, Brown and Black for embroidery
Sewing machine, needle, thead

9 Green prints, Light to Medium

7 Tan prints, Ivory to Tan

continued from page 5

Batik Beauty Quilt

SIZE: 42" x 55"
MATERIALS:
E. E. Schenck Company/Galaxy
Java Batiks
Purchase 1 'Sweet 16s' pack OR 29 fabrics 9" x 11"

4 Dark Navy to Purple	or ¼ yd
3 Lavender/Pink	or ¼ yd
3 Yellow to Lime	or ¼ yd
5 Burgundy to Red	or ½ yd
5 Brown to Gold	or ½ yd
3 Orange to Yellow	or ¼ yd
4 Green to Olive	or ¼ yd
2 Turquoise to Blue	or ¼ yd

Inner Border	Purchase ¼ yd Purple
Binding	Purchase ½ yd Aqua
Backing	Purchase 1½ yds
Batting	Purchase 48" x 59"

Sewing machine, needles, thread

DIVIDE UP THE COLORS:
Block Colors:
Choose the 20 brightest colors for the blocks and strips in the center of the quilt.
Border Colors:
Save 9 pastel or lightest colors for the outer border.

CUTTING:
Blocks and Strips:
Cut each block into 2 pieces (use the 20 brightest colors).

Cut 1 square 9" x 9"

Cut 1 strip 1½" x 8½"

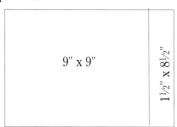

Block Cutting Diagram
Cut 20 squares and 20 strips

MAKE HALF-SQUARE TRIANGLES:
Group Colors into Pairs,
such as Yellow/Yellow, Orange/Orange, Pink/Pink, etc.
At the end you may have a few pair that don't match as well, but it is OK.

See Half-Square Triangle Diagram.
Sew all 20 squares to make 20 Half-Square Triangles.

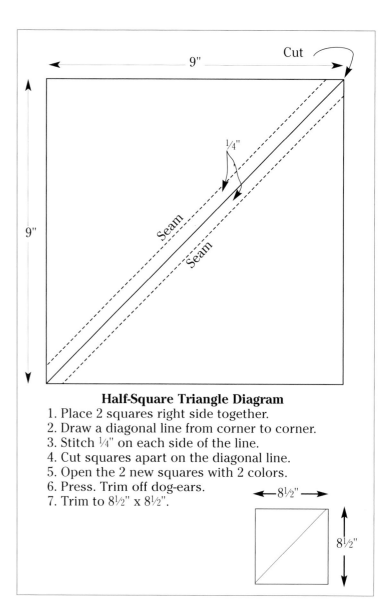

Half-Square Triangle Diagram
1. Place 2 squares right side together.
2. Draw a diagonal line from corner to corner.
3. Stitch ¼" on each side of the line.
4. Cut squares apart on the diagonal line.
5. Open the 2 new squares with 2 colors.
6. Press. Trim off dog-ears.
7. Trim to 8½" x 8½".

Refer to photo for direction of the diagonal and color placement:
Color Placement:
Lay 2-color squares and strips out on a work surface or table.

Position colors as desired.
Note: Divide the quilt visually into 2 triangles. Begin to place colors in the upper left corner of the quilt. Then start in the lower right corner to place the colors in the same sequence.

ASSEMBLY:
Blocks and Strips:
Sew blocks and strips in 4 columns following the Assembly Diagram. Press.
Sew the columns together to make the center of the quilt. Press.

BORDERS:
Dark Inner Border #1:
Cut 2 borders 1½" x 45½" for the sides.
Cut 2 borders 1½" x 34½" for the top and bottom.

Sew side borders to the quilt. Press.
Add the top and bottom borders. Press.

Batik - Quilt Assembly

Light Pieced Outer Border #2:
Cut strips 4½" x 11" (use 8 pastel or light colors).
Randomly sew the strips together end to end.

Cut 2 pieced borders 4½" x 47½" for the sides.
Cut 2 pieced borders 4½" x 34½" for the top and bottom.

Cut 4 squares 4½" x 4½" for the corners (use 1 Light color).

Sew 4½" x 47½" borders to the sides of the quilt. Press.

Sew a 4½" x 4½"square to each end of the 4½" x 34½" top and bottom
    strips to make 4½" x 42½" borders. Press.

Sew the 4½" x 42½" borders to the top and bottom of the quilt. Press.

FINISH:
Quilting:
    See Quilting Basic Instructions on pages 18 - 20.

Binding:
    Cut 2½" strips and sew end to end to make 202".
    Follow Binding Instructions on page 21.

continued from page 7

WillowBerry Basket of Flowers

SIZE: 47" x 47"
MATERIALS:
E. E. Schenck Company/Maywood Studio
WillowBerry Winter by WillowBerry Lane
Purchase 1 'Sweet 16s' pack OR 18 fabrics 9" x 11":

5 Peach prints	or ½ yd
6 Green prints	or ½ yd
5 Ivory/Tan prints	or ½ yd
1 Ivory/Peach stripe	or ¼ yd
1 Red check	or ¼ yd

Border & Binding   Purchase 2¾ yds Peach border print
Backing   Purchase 3 yds
Batting   Purchase 52" x 52"
Sewing machine, needle, thread

CUTTING:

Center Block:
Use 3 of the Lightest prints:
Cut 2 blocks 8" x 11" (use 2 Light prints).
Cut 2 blocks 5" x 8" (use 1 Light print).

Green Inner Border #1:
Cut 4 strips 1½" x 9½" for centers (use 1 Green/floral stripe).
Cut 8 strips 1½" x 3½" for corner strips (use 1 Med. Green).
Cut 4 squares 1½" x 1½" for the corners (use leftover Green).

Green and Pink Border #2:
Cut 16 squares 4½" x 4½" for the Half-Square Triangles
    (use 2 Green print to cut 8 squares and
    2 Peach print to cut 8 squares).
Cut 4 squares 4" x 4" for the corners (use 1 Peach floral).
Cut 4 blocks 4" x 3½" for the centers (use 1 Green floral).

Light Pieced Border #3:
Cut 12 strips 3" x 11" (use 4 Light prints).

Mitered - Floral & Stripe Border Print Outer Border #4:
Cut 4 borders 9½" x 47½".
    NOTE: Think before you cut when using a Border Print.
    Place the Green stripe along the edge of the binding
    and begin your cut ¼" from that line.

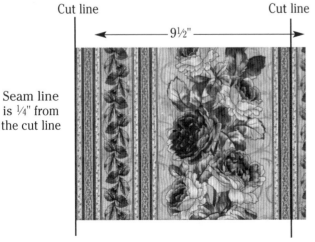

Cutting Diagram for Outer Border #4

ASSEMBLY:
Sew 2 center blocks together
    (8" x 11"and 5" x 8").
    to make a piece
    8" x 15½". Press.
Repeat with the other 2
    center blocks
    (8" x 11" and 5" x 8").
Sew the blocks together
    to make a
    15½" x 15½" square.

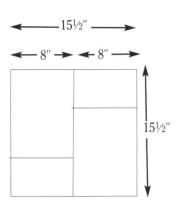

Green Inner Border #1:
Sew strips 1½" x 3½", 1½" x 9½", and 1½" x 3½"
    together end to end for 1½" x 15½".
Make 4 of these 1½" x 15½" borders.

Sew 1½" x 1½" squares to each corner of 2 strips to
    make 1½" x 17½" borders for the top and bottom.

Sew 1½" x 15½" borders to the sides of quilt. Press.
Sew 1½" x 17½" borders to the top and bottom. Press.

Green and Pink Border #2:
MAKE HALF-SQUARE TRIANGLES:
Group Colors into Pairs of Green/Pink.

See Half-Square Triangle Diagram.
    Sew all 16 squares to make 16 Half-Square Triangles.

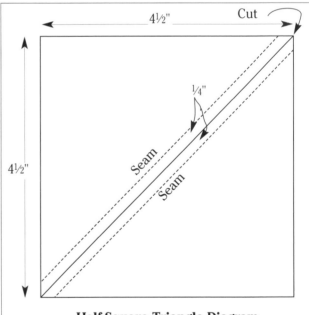

Half-Square Triangle Diagram
1. Place 2 squares right side together.
2. Draw a diagonal line from corner to corner.
3. Stitch ¼" on each side of the line.
4. Cut squares apart on the diagonal line.
5. Open the 2 new squares with 2 colors.
6. Press. Trim off dog-ears.
7. Trim to 4" x 4".

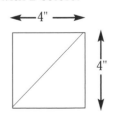

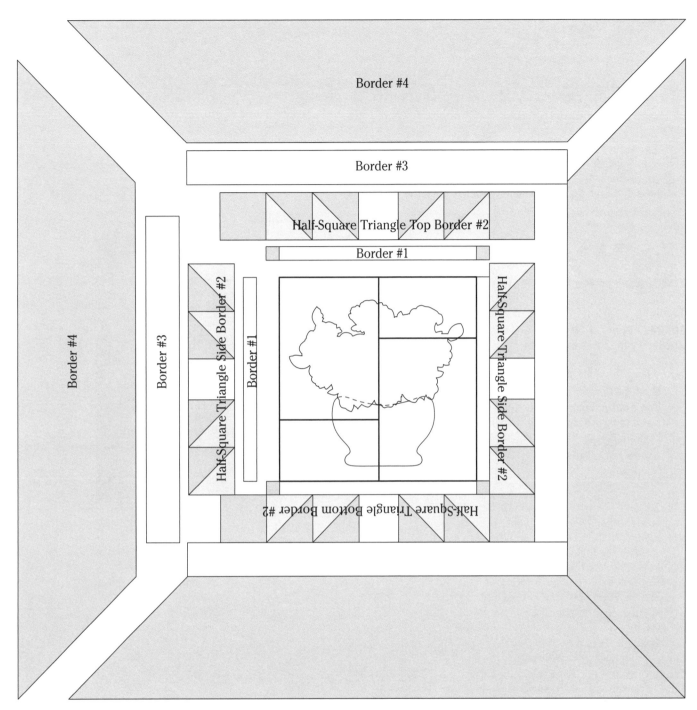

WillowBerry Basket of Flowers - Quilt Assembly

Refer to photo for direction of the diagonal
  and color placement:

Green and Pink Borders:
Sew 2 Half-Square Triangles, a 4" x 3½" rectangle, and
  2 Half-Square Triangles together to form a
  border 4" x 17½". Press.
  Make 4 of these 4" x 17½" borders.

Sew a 4" x 4" square to each corner of 2 borders to make
  4" x 24½" strips for the top and bottom. Press.

Sew 4" x 17½" borders to the sides of the quilt. Press.
Sew 4" x 24½" borders to the top and bottom. Press.

Light Pieced Border #3:
Sew 3" x 11" strips together end to end. Press.

Cut 2 borders 3" x 24½" for the sides of the quilt. Press.
Cut 2 borders 3" x 29½" for the top and bottom. Press.

Sew 3" x 24½" borders to the side of the quilt. Press.
Sew 3" x 29½" borders to the top and bottom. Press.

continued on page 14

continued from page 13

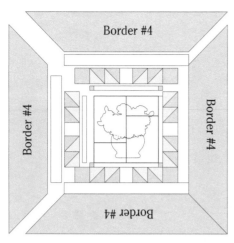

WillowBerry Basket of Flowers - Quilt Assembly

Mitered - Floral & Stripe
Border Print Outer Border #4:
Center a 9½" x 47½" border strip along each
   side of the quilt, allowing 9"
   to hang off the edges for mitering.

Sew borders to the sides of the quilt. Press.
Sew borders to the top and bottom. Press.

Miter the four corners (see below). Press.

APPLIQUE:
Cut out vase using the pattern (use 1 Red check).
Cut out your favorite roses from the Peach
   border scraps leaving a scant ¼" border all
   around. Position the roses in the vase as
   desired. Baste in place.
Applique vase and flowers in place.
See Basic Applique Instructions for
   'Needle Turn Applique' on page 20.

FINISH:
Quilting:
See Quilting Instructions on pages 18 - 20.
Binding:
Cut 2½" strips and sew together end to
   end to make 196".
Follow Binding Instructions on page 21.

WillowBerry Basket of Flowers
Vase Pattern

Mitered Border

Center, pin and
sew borders to the
sides of the quilt.
Stop the seam at
the corner.

Fold the quilt at
a diagonal so the
miter will extend
from the corner
outward.

Pin or baste
miter seam,
carefully lin-
ing up the
pattern.

Use a ruler to draw a line from
the corner out to the edge of
the border. Sew a seam.
TIP: I use a long stitch in case I
need to rip it out and redo it.

Check the miter seam
to be sure it lines up
correctly and lays
down flat, resew it
with a normal stitch.

Trim off excess
fabric under-
neath the cor-
ners. Repeat on
all 4 corners.

continued from page 17

Scallop Quilt Heart

WillowBerry Winter
Center Quilt Heart

Place Patterns on Fold

WillowBerry Winter
Quilt Banner

LOVE Fills OUr HOME

Applique Fabrics:

Center Heart   9" x 11" Dark Peach
Scallop Heart   9" x 11" Medium Peach
Banner   3" x 10" Light Tan
Birds   5" x 9" Medium Peach
Beaks   1" x 2" Medium Tan
DMC pearl cotton Brown, Black

Bird Wing

WillowBerry Winter
Quilt Bird

continued from page 9

Love Fills Our Home

SIZE: 41" x 47"

MATERIALS:

E. E. Schenck Company/Maywood Studio
WillowBerry Basics by WillowBerry Lane
Purchase 1 'Sweet 16s' pack OR 25 fabrics 9" x 11":

9 Peach prints, Light to Dark	or ¾ yd
9 Green prints, Light to Medium	or ¾ yd
7 Tan prints, Ivory to Tan	or ½ yd

Border & Binding	Purchase 1½ yds Peach print
Backing	Purchase 1¾ yds
Batting	Purchase 45" x 51"

Purchase *DMC* pearl cotton, Brown and Black for embroidery
Sewing machine, needle, thread

CUTTING:

Center block:
Cut 2 blocks 8½" x 10½" (use 2 Light Peach).

Tan Pieced Inner Border #1:
Cut 6 strips 1½" x 11" (use 1 Medium Tan).

Green Pieced Border #2:
Cut 24 squares 3½" x 3½" (use 4 Medium Green).

Peach Pieced Border #3:
Cut 20 squares 4½" x 4½" for the Half-Square Triangles
(use 2 Light Peach to cut 6 Light and
3 Medium Peach to cut 10 Medium and
1 Dark Peach to cut 4 Dark squares).
Cut 4 squares 4" x 4" for the corners (use 1 Light Tan).

Center Filler Blocks (use 1 Light Peach):
Cut 2 rectangles 4" x 3½" for the center sides.
Cut 2 rectangles 4" x 4½" for the center top and bottom.

Light Green Pieced Border #4:
Cut 4 squares 3" x 3" for corners (use 1 Medium Peach).

Cut 26 strips 3" x 5½" (use 5 Light Green).

Medium Green Pieced Border #5:
Cut 14 strips 1½" x 11" (use 3 Medium Green).

Peach Outer Border #6:
Cut 2 borders 5" x 38½" for the sides.
Cut 2 borders 5" x 41½" for the top and bottom.

ASSEMBLY:

Sew the two 8½" x 10½" Light Peach blocks together to
make a piece 10½" x 16½" for the center. Press.

BORDERS:

Tan Pieced Inner Border #1:
Sew 1½" x 11" strips end to end.

Cut 2 borders 1½" x 10½" for the top and bottom.
Sew 1½" x 10½" borders to the top and bottom. Press.

Cut 2 borders 1½" x 18½" for the sides.
Sew 1½" x 18½" borders to the sides of the quilt. Press.

Green Pieced Border #2:
Make 4 borders 3½" x 18½" by sewing 6 squares 3½" x 3½"
into a strip 3½" x 18½". Press.

Sew 3½" x 18½" borders to the sides of the quilt. Press.
Sew 3½" x 18½" borders to the top and bottom. Press.

Peach Pieced Border #3:

MAKE HALF-SQUARE TRIANGLES:

Group Colors into Pairs,
such as Light/Medium, Medium/Dark, etc.

See Half-Square Triangle Diagram.
Sew all 20 squares 4½" x 4½" to make 20 Half-Square Triangles.

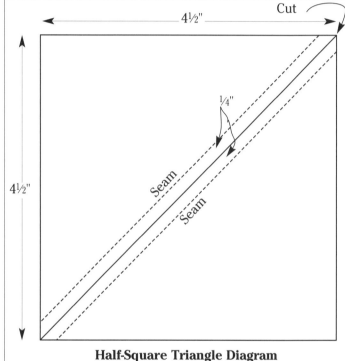

Half-Square Triangle Diagram
1. Place 2 squares right side together.
2. Draw a diagonal line from corner to corner.
3. Stitch ¼" on each side of the line.
4. Cut squares apart on the diagonal line.
5. Open the 2 new squares with 2 colors.
6. Press. Trim off dog-ears.
7. Trim to 4" x 4".

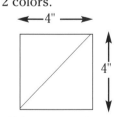

Refer to photo for direction of the diagonal and color placement:

Side Borders - Make 2:
Sew 3 Half-Square Triangles, a 4" x 3½" rectangle, and 3 Half-Square
Triangles to form a border strip 4" x 24½". Press.

Sew 4" x 24½" borders to the sides of the quilt. Press.

Top and Bottom Borders - Make 2:
Sew 2 Half-Square Triangles, a 4" x 4½" rectangle, and 2 Half-Square
Triangles to form a border strip 4⅛" x 18½". Press.
Sew a 4" x 4" square to each end to make 4" x 25½". Press.

Sew 4" x 25½" borders to the top and bottom of the quilt. Press.

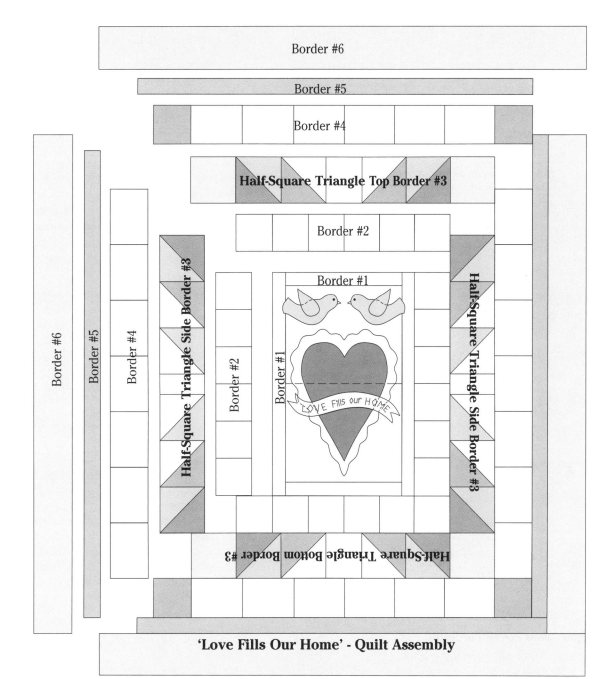

'Love Fills Our Home' - Quilt Assembly

Light Green Pieced Border #4:

Sew 3" x 5½"strips end to end. Press.

Cut 2 borders 3" x 31½" for the sides. Press.

Cut 2 borders 3" x 25½" for the top and bottom. Press.

Sew 3" x 31½" borders to the sides of the quilt. Press.

Sew a 3" x 3" square to each end of the 3" x 25½" border
    to make a border 3" x 30½". Press.

Sew 3" x 30½" borders to the top and bottom. Press.

Medium Green Pieced Border #5:

Sew 1½" x 11" strips end to end.

Cut 2 borders 1½" x 36½" for the sides.

Cut 2 borders 1½" x 32½" for the top and bottom.

Sew 1½" x 36½" borders to the sides of the quilt. Press.

Sew 1½" x 32½" borders to the top and bottom. Press.

Peach Outer Border #6:

Sew 5" x 38½" borders to the sides. Press.

Sew 5" x 41½" borders to the top and bottom. Press.

APPLIQUES:

Use the patterns on page 15.

Cut out pieces leaving a ⅛" border all around. Prepare
pieces for 'Needle Turn Appliqué' using your favorite
method. See Applique Basic Instructions on page 20.

To make the bird beaks, cut a 1" square of fabric and fold it
into a triangle until you like the look.

Position all pieces and baste in place.

Place the beak under the bird and appliqué it first.

Appliqué all other pieces.

Embroider the letters with Brown Straight Stitches.

Embroider eyes on birds with Black French Knots.

FINISH:

Quilting: See Quilting Basic Instructions on pages 18 - 20.

Binding: Cut 2½" strips and sew together end to end
    to make 184".
    Follow Binding Instructions on page 21.

Design Tips
with 'Sweet 16s'

I love quilting with 'Sweet 16s' collections of 9" x 11" fabric pieces. With 'Sweet 16s' you get a wonderful scrappy look.

I want to share a few tips for working with 'Sweet 16s'. The colors are always beautiful together and create the handmade scrappy look that is so popular today.

My first step in designing is to divide the 9" x 11" pieces into groups of color... Greens, Purples, Browns, Tans, etc. Next I estimate the number of pieces I will need for the blocks and borders in the quilt.

Sometimes I need an extra piece or two of a color, let's say Green so I look for a Tan print with a lot of Green and move it to the Green stack.... and the same with other colors.

Enjoy quilting...

Suzanne McNeill

Tips for Working with 9" x 11" Cuts
TIPS: As a Guide for Yardage:
Each 1/4 yard or a 'Fat 1/16 yard' equals a 9" x 11" piece.
A pre-cut 'Sweet 16s' piece is 9" x 11".

Pre-cut 9" x 11" pieces are usually cut on the crosswise grain and are prone to stretching. These tips will help reduce stretching and make your quilt lay flat for quilting.

1. When sewing crosswise grain strips together, take care not to stretch the strips. If you detect any puckering as you go, rip out the seam and sew it again.

2. Press, Do Not Iron. Carefully open fabric, with the seam to one side, press without moving the iron. A back-and-forth ironing motion stretches the fabric.

3. Reduce the wiggle in your borders with this technique from garment making.

First, accurately cut your borders to the exact measure of the quilt top.

Then, before sewing the border to the quilt, run a double row of stay stitches along the outside edge to maintain the original shape and prevent stretching.

Pin the border to the quilt, taking care not to stretch the quilt top to make it fit. Pinning reduces slipping and stretching.

Rotary Cutting Tips

Rotary Cutter: Friend or Foe

A rotary cutter is a wonderful and useful tool. When not used correctly, the sharp blade can be dangerous. Follow these safety tips:

1. Never cut toward you.

2. Use a sharp blade. Pressing harder on a dull blade can cause the blade to jump the ruler and injure your fingers.

3. Always disengage the blade before the cutter leaves your hand, even if you intend to pick it up immediately.

Rotary cutters have been caught when lifting fabric, have fallen onto the floor and have cut fingers.

Basic Cutting Instructions

Tips for Accurate Cutting:

Accurate cutting is easy when using a rotary cutter with a sharp blade, a cutting mat, and a transparent ruler. Begin by pressing your fabric and then follow these steps:

1. Folding:

a) Fold the fabric with the selvage edges together. Smooth the fabric flat. If needed, fold again to make your fabric length smaller than the length of the ruler.

b) Align the fold with one of the guide lines on the mat. This is important to avoid getting a kink in your strip.

2. Cutting:

a) Align the ruler with a guide line on the mat. Press down on the ruler to prevent it shifting or have someone help hold the ruler. Hold the rotary cutter along the edge of the ruler and cut off the selvage edge.

b) Also using the guide line on the mat, cut the ends straight.

c) Strips for making the quilt top may be cut on 'crosswise grain' (from selvage to selvage) or 'on grain' (parallel to the selvage edge).

Strips for borders should be cut on grain (parallel to the selvage edge) to prevent wavy edges and make quilting easier.

d) When cutting strips, move the ruler, NOT the fabric.

Basic Sewing Instructions

You now have precisely cut strips that are exactly the correct width. You are well on your way to blocks that fit together perfectly. Accurate sewing is the next important step.

Matching Edges:

1. Carefully line up the edges of your strips. Many times, if the underside is off a little, your seam will be off by ⅛". This does not sound like much until you have 8 seams in a block, each off by ⅛". Now your finished block is a whole inch wrong!

2. Pin the pieces together to prevent them shifting.

Seam Allowance:

I cannot stress enough the importance of accurate ¼" seams. All the quilts in this book are measured for ¼" seams unless otherwise indicated.

Most sewing machine manufacturers offer a Quarter-inch foot. A Quarter-inch foot is the most worthwhile investment you can make in your quilting.

Pressing:

I want to talk about pressing even before we get to sewing because proper pressing can make the difference between a quilt that wins a ribbon at the quilt show and one that does not.

Press, do NOT iron. What does that mean? Many of us want to move the iron back and forth along the seam. This "ironing" stretches the strip out of shape and creates errors that accumulate as the quilt is constructed. Believe it or not, there is a correct way to press your seams, and here it is:

1. Do NOT use steam with your iron. If you need a little water, spritz it on.

2. Place your fabric flat on the ironing board without opening the seam. Set a hot iron on the seam and count to 3. Lift the iron and move to the next position along the seam. Repeat until the entire seam is pressed. This sets and sinks the threads into the fabric.

3. Now, carefully lift the top strip and fold it away from you so the seam is on one side. Usually the seam is pressed toward the darker fabric, but often the direction of the seam is determined by the piecing requirements.

4. Press the seam open with your fingers. Add a little water or spray starch if it wants to close again. Lift the iron and place it on the seam. Count to 3. Lift the iron again and continue until the seam is pressed. Do NOT use the tip of the iron to push the seam open. So many people do this and wonder later why their blocks are not fitting together.

5. Most critical of all: For accuracy every seam must be pressed before the next seam is sewn.

Working with 'Crosswise Grain' strips:

Strips cut on the crosswise grain (from selvage to selvage) have problems similar to bias edges and are prone to stretching. To reduce stretching and make your quilt lay flat for quilting, keep these tips in mind.

1. Take care not to stretch the strips as you sew.

2. Adjust the sewing thread tension and the presser foot pressure if needed.

3. If you detect any puckering as you go, rip out the seam and sew it again. It is much easier to take out a seam now than to do it after the block is sewn.

Sewing Bias Edges:

Bias edges wiggle and stretch out of shape very easily. They are not recommended for beginners, but even a novice can accomplish bias edges if these techniques are employed.

1. Stabilize the bias edge with one of these methods:

   a) Press with spray starch.

   b) Press freezer paper or removable iron-on stabilizer to the back of the fabric.

   c) Sew a double row of stay stitches along the bias edge and ⅛" from the bias edge. This is a favorite technique of garment makers.

2. Pin, pin, pin! I know many of us dislike pinning, but when working with bias edges, pinning makes the difference between intersections that match and those that do not.

Building Better Borders:

Wiggly borders make a quilt very difficult to finish. However, wiggly borders can be avoided with these techniques.

1. Cut the borders on grain. That means cutting your strips parallel to the selvage edge.

2. Accurately cut your borders to the exact measure of the quilt.

3. If your borders are piece stripped from crosswise grain fabrics, press well with spray starch and sew a double row of stay stitches along the outside edge to maintain the original shape and prevent stretching.

4. Pin the border to the quilt, taking care not to stretch the quilt top to make it fit. Pinning reduces slipping and stretching.

Basic Applique Instructions

Basic Turned Edge

1. Trace pattern onto template plastic.

2. Cut out the shape leaving a scant ¼" fabric border all around and clip the curves.

3. Place the template plastic on the wrong side of the fabric. Spray edges with starch.

4. Press the ⅛" border over the edge of the template plastic with the tip of a hot iron. Press firmly.

5. Remove the template, maintaining the folded edge on the back of the fabric.

6. Position the shape on the quilt and Blindstitch in place.

Basic Needle Turn

1. Cut out the shape leaving a ¼" fabric border all around.

2. Baste the shapes to the quilt, keeping the basting stitches away from the edge of the fabric.

3. Begin with all areas that are under other layers and work to the topmost layer.

4. For an area no more than 2" ahead of where you are working, trim to ⅛" and clip the curves.

5. Using the needle, roll the edge under and sew tiny Blindstitches to secure.

Using Fusible Web for Iron-on Applique:

1. Trace the pattern onto *Steam a Seam 2* fusible web.

2. Press the patterns onto the wrong side of the fabric.

3. Cut out patterns exactly on the drawn line.

4. Score the web paper with a pin, then remove the paper.

5. Position the fabric, fusible side down, on the quilt. Press with a hot iron following the fusible web manufacturer's instructions.

6. Stitch around the edge by hand.

Optional: Stabilize the wrong side of the fabric with your favorite stabilizer.

Use a size 80 machine embroidery needle. Fill the bobbin with lightweight basting thread and thread the machine with a machine embroidery thread that complements the color being appliqued.

Set your machine for a Zigzag stitch and adjust the thread tension if needed. Use a scrap to experiment with different stitch widths and lengths until you find the one you like best.

Sew slowly.

Basic Layering Instructions

Marking Your Quilt:

If you choose to mark your quilt for hand or machine quilting, it is much easier to do so before layering. Press your quilt before you begin. Here are some handy tips regarding marking.

1. A disappearing pen may vanish before you finish.

2. Use a White pencil on dark fabrics.

3. If using a washable Blue pen, remember that pressing may make the pen permanent.

Pieced Backings:

1. Press the backing fabric before measuring.

2. If possible cut backing fabrics on grain, parallel to the selvage edges.

3. Piece 3 parts rather than 2 whenever possible, sewing 2 side borders to the center. This reduces stress on the pieced seam.

4. The backing and batting should extend at least 2" on each side of the quilt.

Creating a Quilt Sandwich:

1. Press the backing and top to remove all wrinkles.

2. Lay the backing wrong side up on the table.

3. Position the batting over the backing and smooth out all wrinkles.

4. Center the quilt top over the batting leaving a 2" border all around.

5. Pin the layers together with 2" safety pins positioned a handwidth apart. A grapefruit spoon makes inserting the pins easier. Leaving the pins open in the container speeds up the basting on the next quilt.

Basic Quilting Instructions

Hand Quilting:

Many quilters enjoy the serenity of hand quilting. Because the quilt is handled a great deal, it is important to securely baste the sandwich together. Place the quilt in a hoop and don't forget to hide your knots.

Machine Quilting:

All the quilts in this book were machine quilted. Some were quilted on a large, free-arm quilting machine and others were quilted on a sewing machine. If you have never machine quilted before, practice on some scraps first.

Straight Line Machine Quilting Tips:

1. Pin baste the layers securely.

2. Set up your sewing machine with a size 80 quilting needle and a walking foot.

3. Experimenting with the decorative stitches on your machine adds interest to your quilt. You do not have to quilt the entire piece with the same stitch. Variety is the spice of life, so have fun trying out stitches you have never used before as well as your favorite stand-bys.

Free Motion Machine Quilting Tips:

1. Pin baste the layers securely.

2. Set up your sewing machine with a spring needle, a quilting foot, and lower the feed dogs.

Basic Mitered Binding
Instructions

A Perfect Finish:

The binding endures the most stress on a quilt and is usually the first thing to wear out. For this reason, we recommend using a double fold binding.

1. Trim the backing and batting even with the quilt edge.

2. If possible cut strips on the crosswise grain because a little bias in the binding is a Good thing. This is the only place in the quilt where bias is helpful, for it allows the binding to give as it is turned to the back and sewn in place.

3. Strips are usually cut 2½" wide, but check the instructions for your project before cutting.

4. Sew strips end to end to make a long strip sufficient to go all around the quilt plus 4"- 6".

5. With wrong sides together, fold the strip in half lengthwise. Press.

6. Stretch out your hand and place your little finger at the corner of the quilt top. Place the binding where your thumb touches the edge of the quilt. Aligning the edge of the quilt with the raw edges of the binding, pin the binding in place along the first side.

7. Leaving a 2" tail for later use, begin sewing the binding to the quilt with a ¼" seam.

For Mitered Corners:

1. Stop ¼" from the first corner. Leave the needle in the quilt and turn it 90°. Hit the reverse button on your machine and back off the quilt leaving the threads connected.

2. Fold the binding perpendicular to the side you sewed, making a 45° angle. Carefully maintaining the first fold, bring the binding back along the edge to be sewn.

3. Carefully align the edges of the binding with the quilt edge and sew as you did the first side. Repeat this process until you reach the tail left at the beginning. Fold the tail out of the way and sew until you are ¼" from the beginning stitches.

4. Remove the quilt from the machine. Fold the quilt out of the way and match the binding tails together. Carefully sew the binding tails with a ¼" seam. You can do this by hand if you prefer.

Finishing the Binding:

5. Trim the seam to reduce bulk.

6. Finish stitching the binding to the quilt across the join you just sewed.

7. Turn the binding to the back of the quilt. To reduce bulk at the corners, fold the miter in the opposite direction from which it was folded on the front.

8. Hand-sew a Blind stitch on the back of the quilt to secure the binding in place.

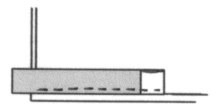

Align the raw edge of the binding with the raw edge of the quilt top. Start about 8" from the corner and go along the first side with a ¼" seam.

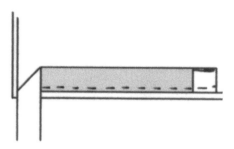

Stop ¼" from the edge. Then stitch a slant to the corner (through both layers of binding)... lift up, then down, as you line up the edge. Fold the binding back.

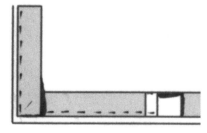

Align the raw edges again. Continue stitching the next side with a ¼" seam as you sew the binding in place.

continued from page 31

ASSEMBLY:
Follow the Quilt Assembly Diagram.
Sew 6 rectangles together to form each row. Press.
Make 6 rows.

Hydrangea Quilt

SIZE: 46" x 54"

MATERIALS:
E. E. Schenck Company/Maywood Studio
Hydrangea by Glenna Hailey
Purchase 1 'Sweet 16s' pack OR 32 fabrics 9" x 11"

5 Pink prints	or ½ yd
5 Blue prints	or ½ yd
5 Yellow prints	or ½ yd
5 Green prints	or ½ yd
12 White prints	or ½ yd

Border & Binding	Purchase 1 yd Green print
Backing	Purchase 2 yds
Batting	Purchase 52" x 60"

Sewing machine, needle, thread

CUTTING:
Cut 12 rectangles 8½" x 10½" for the blocks:
 (use 3 Yellow, 3 Green, 3 Pink, 3 Blue)
Cut 24 rectangles 5½" x 8½" for the smaller blocks:
 (use 2 Yellow, 2 Green, 2 Pink, 2 Blue, 4 White print)

Green Inner Border:
Cut 2 borders 1½" x 48½" for the sides. Press.
Cut 2 borders 1½" x 42½" for the top and bottom. Press.

White Outer Pieced Border:
Cut 24 White 2½" x 9" strips (use 6 White print fabrics).

Row 1: Blue | Blue | White | Pink | Pink | White

Row 2: Blue | Yellow | Blue | Pink | Green | Pink

Row 3: White | Blue | Blue | White | Pink | Pink

Row 4: Green | Green | White | Yellow | Yellow | White

Row 5: Green | Pink | Green | Yellow | Blue | Yellow

Row 6: White | Green | Green | White | Yellow | Yellow

Sew the rows together to make the center of the quilt. Press.

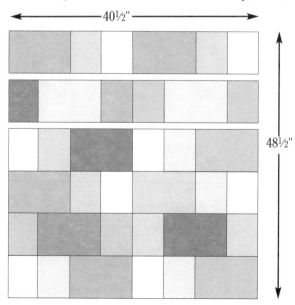

◄— 40½" —►

48½"

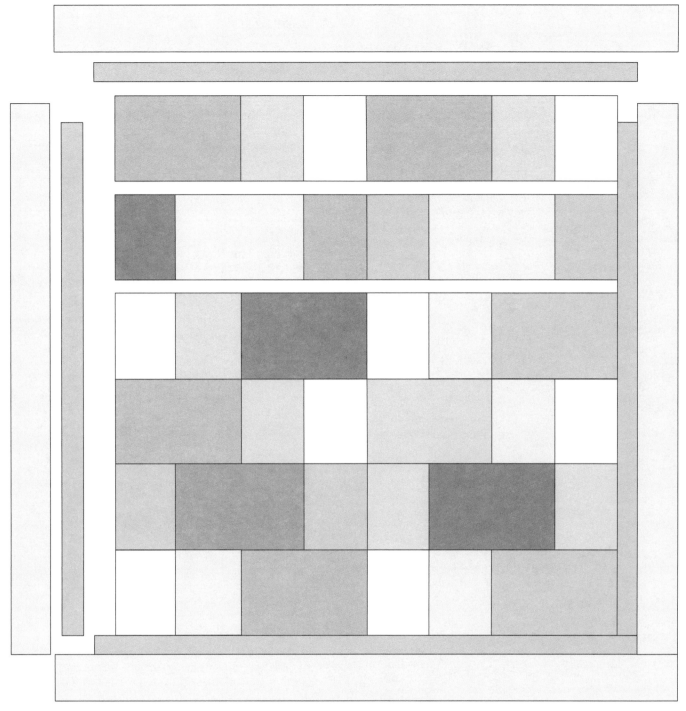

Hydrangea Quilt Assembly

BORDERS:

Inner Border #1:
Sew Green 1½" x 48½" borders to the sides. Press.
Sew Green 1½" x 42½" borders to top and bottom. Press.

White Outer Pieced Border #2:
Sew White print 2½" x 9" strips together end to end.

Cut 2 borders 2½" x 50½" for the sides of the quilt. Press.
Cut 2 borders 2½" x 46½". Press.

Sew White print 2½" x 50½" borders to the sides. Press.
Sew White print 2½" x 46½" borders to top and bottom. Press.

FINISH:
Quilting:
See Quilting Basic Instructions on pages 18 - 20.
Binding:
Cut 2½" strips and sew together end to end
to make 208".
Follow Binding Instructions on page 21.

continued from page 33

Fuchsia Quilt

SIZE: 49" x 60½"
NOTE: This quilt is more advanced, not for beginners.

BEFORE YOU BEGIN:

Although this quilt is a little tricky, it actually has repetitous blocks that form an 'optical illusion' of a 'waterfall' as the colors flow down. The tricky part is color placement, refer to the photo carefully.

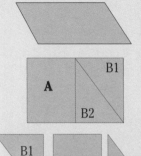

It helps to understand the 'illusion' block. Each color looks like an unusual shape in the finished quilt because the 2 seams are invisible after it is quilted.

1. First: cut each 9" x 11" piece into 3 smaller pieces, A, B1 and B2.

After cutting, move the pieces into position as you layout the quilt (refer to the photo).

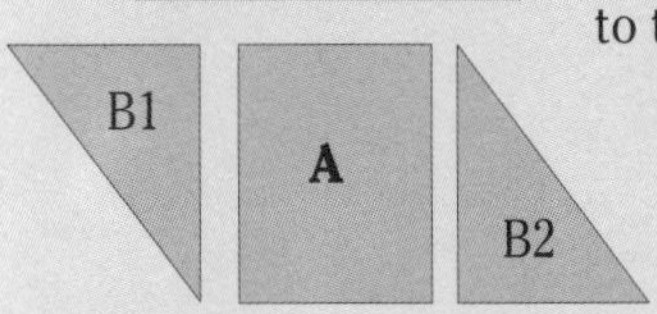

2. Next: pair a B1 with a (B2), of another color. Sew these triangles together. Trim to 5" x 8½".

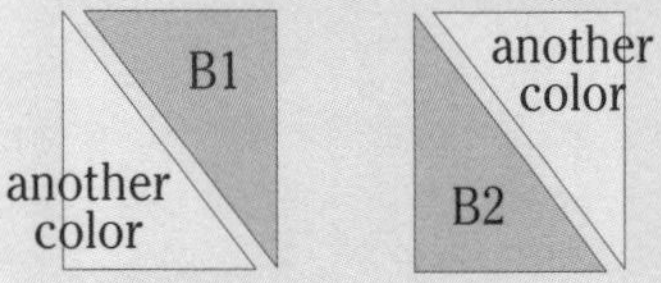

3. Now: pair B2 with a (B1) of another color. Sew these blocks together and trim to 5" x 8½".

4. Next: sew B1-(B2), A and B2-(B1) together side to side to create the 'optical illusion' block.

Finally: sew the blocks together in rows to create the 'waterfall' effect.

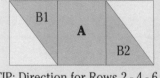

TIP: Direction for Rows 2 - 4 - 6.

TIP: Rows 3 - 5 - (7-1) are → oriented the other direction.

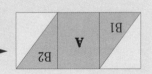

MATERIALS:
E. E. Schenck Company/Maywood Studio
Fuchsia by Jackie Robinson
Purchase 1 'Sweet 16s' pack OR 24 fabrics 9" x 11"

6 Cream to Tan prints	or ¼ yd each
6 Red to Fuschia	or ¼ yd each
6 Yellow to Green	or ¼ yd each
6 Lavender to Purple	or ¼ yd each

Border #1 & Binding	Purchase 1 yd Dark Green
Border #2	Purchase 2 yds Dark Purple
Backing	Purchase 2⅛ yds
Batting	Purchase 54" x 66"

Sewing machine, needle, thread

CUTTING:
Rectangles for Rows 1 - 7:
B - Cut 5½" x 9" rectangles
   Make 24 (1 each) of 6 colors in each of 4 color groups:
   Lavender to Purple
   Yellow to Green
   Red to Fuschia
   Cream to Tan

A - Cut 5" x 8½" rectangles
   Make 24 (1 each) of 6 colors in each of 4 color groups:

C - Cut **only** 6 Cream to Tan 5½" x 9" rectangles into 12 2¾" x 8½" for Columns 1 and 9. **Note: 2¾" wide.**

B - 5½" x 9" Make 24 (1 each) of 6 colors in each of 4 color groups into Split Rectangles (see below). for Columns 2 - 4 - 6 - 8	**A - 5" x 8½"** Save 24 (1 each) of 6 colors in each of 4 color groups. for Columns 1 - 3 - 5 - 7 - 9	**C - 2¾" x 8½"** Cut 12 Cream to Tan for Columns 1 and 9

Rectangles Cutting Diagrams

Split-Rectangle Triangles for Rows 1 - 7:
IMPORTANT NOTE:
With Split-Rectangle Triangles you must cut first and then sew.
Use 24 (1 each) of 6 colors in each of 4 color groups.
Be sure all fabrics are right side up so the diagonal will be correct.
Draw a line diagonally from corner to corner.
Cut on the line.

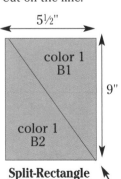

Split-Rectangle Triangles Cutting Diagram

Follow the Split- Rectangle Triangle Cutting Diagram.

Cut the Stack so all 24 rectangles form 2 parts of a Block B (with left and right triangles).

Note: Divide up the stack and cut only 4 layers at a time.

Cut on the diagonal line.

Carefully refer to color placement in **columns 2 - 4 - 6 - 8**.
   Pair the fabric colors with right sides together.
Pair up 24 **B** triangles, for Rows 3 - 5 - (7-1) & 2 - 4 - 6. Press.

Line up the raw edges ¼" from the corners.

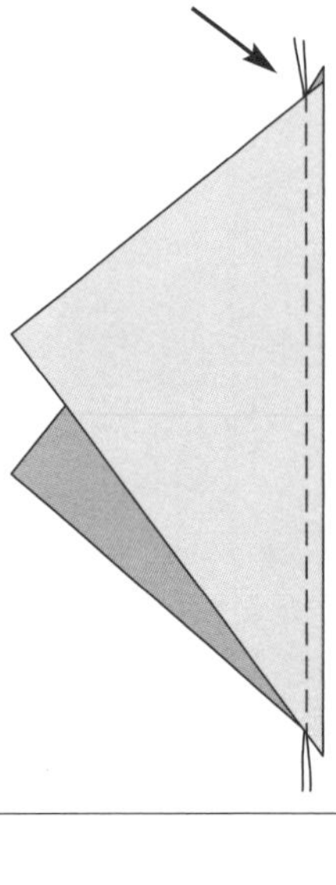

Carefully line up 2 Split-triangles along the diagonal. With right sides together, line up the corners so the seam will begin at a raw edge of both fabrics.

Sew ¼" from the diagonal edge of each pair. Press.

Trim each sewn 'B' to 5" x 8½"

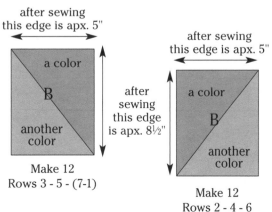

Split-Rectangle Triangle Sewing Diagrams

SEWING:

Sew the Split-Rectangle Triangles.
See instructions in the box.

ASSEMBLY:

Arrange the blocks in rows following
the Quilt Assembly Diagram.

Rows 2 - 6: Use the Darker colors in
each group. Pay close attention to
the direction of the diagonal and the
color placement.

Sew all blocks together to form
Rows 2 - 6. Press.

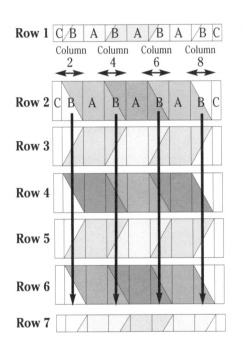

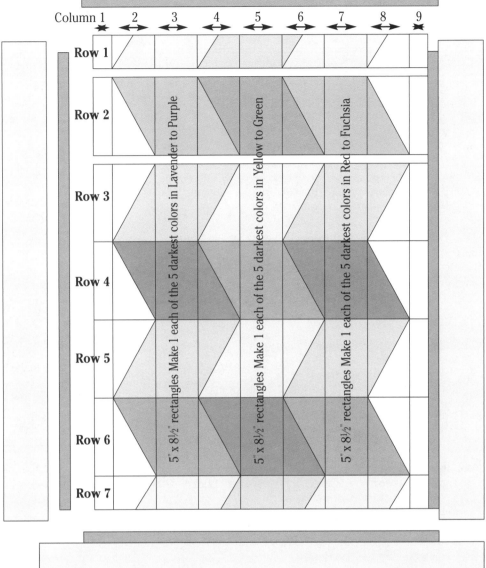

Fuchsia - Quilt Assembly

Arrange the blocks in a row following the illustration above.

Rows 1 and 7: Use the Light colors in each group. Pay close
attention to the direction of the diagonal and the color placement.

Sew all blocks together to form **one row** 8½" x 36½". Press.

Cut the row apart down the center to form 2 rows 4¼" x 36½".

Center of the Quilt:

Sew all rows (1 - 7) together to make the center of the quilt. Press.

BORDERS:
Green Inner Border #1:
Cut 2 borders 1½" x 48" for the sides.
Cut 2 borders 1½" x 38½" for the top and bottom

Sew borders 1½" x 48" to the sides.
Sew borders 1½" x 38½" to the top and bottom. Press.

Purple Outer Border #2:
Cut 2 borders 6" x 50" for the sides.
Cut 2 borders 6" x 49½" for the top and bottom

Sew borders 6" x 50" to the sides. Press.
Sew borders 6" x 49½" to the top and bottom. Press.

FINISH:
Quilting: See Quilting Basic Instructions on page 18 - 20.
Binding: Cut 2½" strips and sew together end to end
to make 230".
Follow Binding Instructions on page 21.

continued from page 35

Sugar and Spice

SIZE: 41" x 41"

MATERIALS:

E. E. Schenck Company/Maywood Studio
Sugar 'N Spice by Glenna Hailey

Purchase 1 'Sweet 16s' pack OR 20 fabrics 9" x 11":

6 White prints	or ½ yd
2 White/Red floral	or ¼ yd
3 Yellow prints	or ¼ yd
2 Dark Green prints	or ¼ yd
3 Medium Green prints	or ¼ yd
2 Dark Red prints	or ¼ yd
2 Medium Red prints	or ¼ yd

Outer Border & Binding	Purchase 1¼ yds Red print
Backing	Purchase 1½ yds
Batting	Purchase 46" x 46"

Sewing machine, needle, thread

CUTTING:

Center Block - Background for House:

Cut 2 rectangles 4" x 5" for A (use 1 White/Red floral).
Cut 2 rectangles 4" x 5" for B (use 1 White print).
Cut 2 rectangles 5" x 8" for E (use 1 White print).
Cut 2 rectangles 4" x 5" for F (use 1 White print).
Cut 2 background templates, #2 and #4 (page 29) (use 1 White).

Roof and House:

Cut 2 rectangles 5" x 7½" for C and D (use 2 Red print and save excess fabric for borders).
Cut out roof parts using templates #1, 3, 5 (pgs 28-29) (use 1 Dark Green print and 1 Red print. Cut template against the edge to save excess fabric for the windows and borders).

Pieced Border #1:

Cut 4 squares 4½" x 4½" (use 1 White print).
Cut 8 rectangles 4½" x 9½" (use 4 Yellow prints).

Half-Square Triangle Border #2:

Cut 4 squares 4" x 4" (use leftover White/Red floral).
Cut 4 rectangles 4" x 5½" (use 1 Dark Green print).
Cut 8 squares 4" x 4" (use 1 Green print).

Cut 8 squares 4½" x 4½" for half-square triangles (use 2 Green prints).
Cut 8 squares 4½" x 4½" for half-square triangles (use leftover Red prints).

Outer Border #3:

Cut 2 borders 4½" x 33½" for the sides.
Cut 2 borders 4½" x 41½" for the top and bottom.

Green Appliques:

Use leftover Dark Green:
Cut 1 Door 2" x 4½".
Cut 1 Window 2½" x 3".

ASSEMBLY:

Background:

Row 1 - Sew block #F to #F to #F to #F. Press.

Roof:

Sew White (#2) to Red (#1). Press.
Sew Green (#5) to Red (#1). Press.
Sew Green (#3) to White (#4). Press.
Trim each roof section to 5" x 8".

Row 2 - Sew block #E to #2-1-5 to #3-4 to #E. Press.

House:

Sew block #A to #B. Press.
Make another block #A to #B. Press.
Sew block #C to #D. Press.

Row 3 - Sew block #A-B to #C-D to another #A-B. Press.

Center Block:

Sew Row 1 to Row 2 to Row 3, matching the seams. Press.

BORDERS:

Pieced Border #1:

Sew two 4½" x 9½" Yellow strips end to end. Press.
Make 4 sets of 4½" x 18½" Yellow strips.

Sew a border 4½" x 18½" to the sides of the quilt. Press.
Sew a 4½" x 4½" square to each end of two 4½" x 18½" borders to make borders 4½" x 26½". Press.
Sew 4½" x 26½" borders to the top and bottom. Press.
TIP: Choose a Yellow floral for the bottom border.

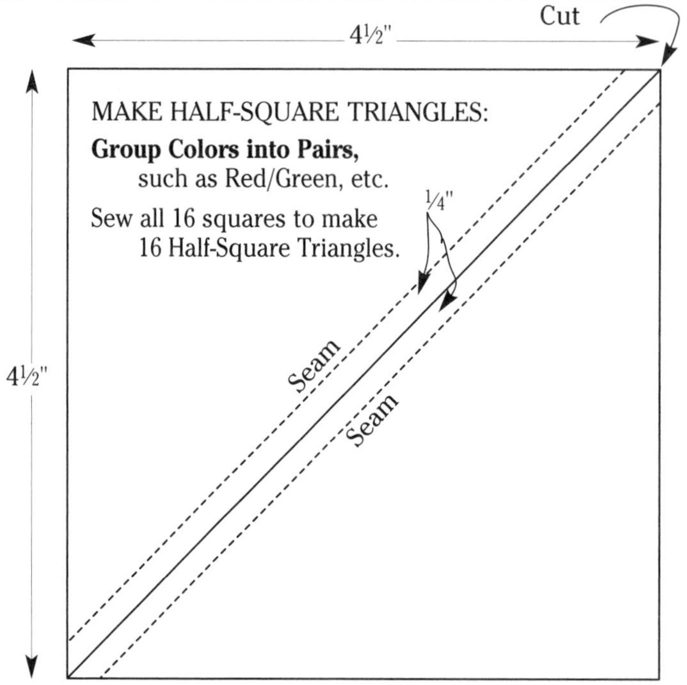
Cut
4½"
4½"
MAKE HALF-SQUARE TRIANGLES:
Group Colors into Pairs,
such as Red/Green, etc.
Sew all 16 squares to make
16 Half-Square Triangles.
¼"
Seam
Seam

Half-Square Triangle Diagram

1. Place 2 squares right side together.
2. Draw a diagonal line from corner to corner.
3. Stitch ¼" on each side of the line.
4. Cut squares apart on the diagonal line.
5. Open the 2 new squares with 2 colors.
6. Press. Trim off dog-ears.
7. Trim to 4" x 4".

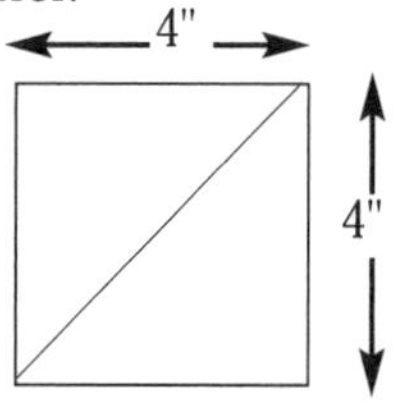
4"
4"

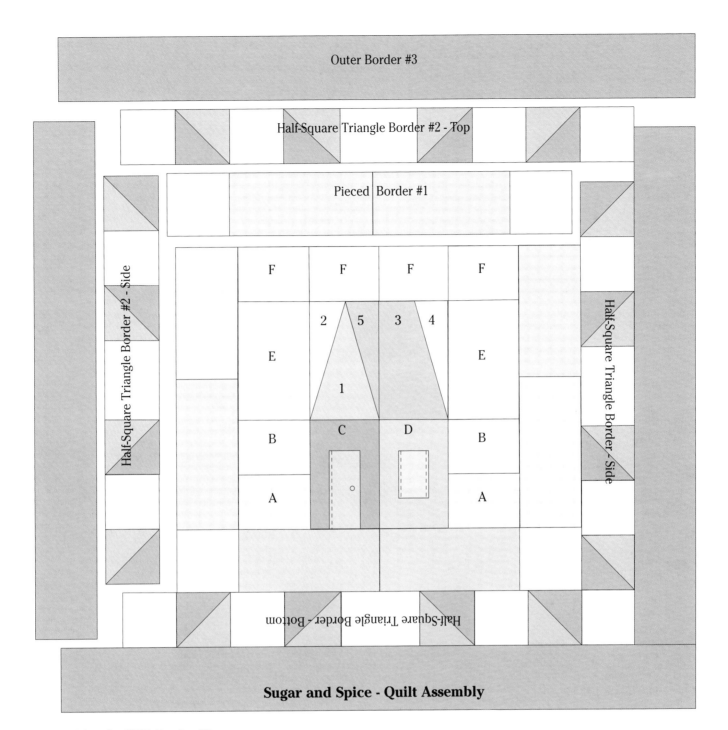

Sugar and Spice - Quilt Assembly

The diagram shows the quilt assembly layout including: Outer Border #3, Half-Square Triangle Border #2 - Top, Pieced Border #1, Half-Square Triangle Border #2 - Side, Half-Square Triangle Border - Side, Half-Square Triangle Border - Bottom, and the central house block with pieces labeled F, E, B, A, C, D, and numbered pieces 1, 2, 3, 4, 5.

Half-Square Triangle (HST) Border #2:

Refer to photo
> for direction of the diagonal and color placement:

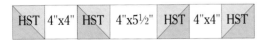

Half-Square Triangle (HST) Border Strips:

Sew sets of Half-Square Triangle Border Strips to make 4 borders, each 4" x 26½". Press

Sew 4" x 26½" borders to the sides of the quilt. Press.

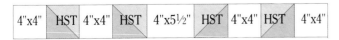

Sew a 4" x 4" square to each end of the 4" x 26½" borders to make borders 4" x 33½". Press.

Sew 4" x 33½" borders to the top and bottom of the quilt. Press.

Red Outer Border #3:

Sew 4½" x 33½" borders to the sides of the quilt. Press.
Sew 4½" x 41½" borders to the top and bottom. Press.

APPLIQUE:
Press a ¼" seam under all around the door.
Press a ¼" seam under all around the window.
Blindstitch door and window to the house.

FINISH:
Quilting: See Quilting Basic Instructions on page 18 - 20.
Binding: Cut 2½" strips and sew together end to end to make 172".
Follow Binding Instructions on page 21.

continued on pages 28 - 29

continued from page 27

Sugar and Spice - Quilt Assembly

Sugar and Spice House
Roof
Pattern 3
Cut 1 Green

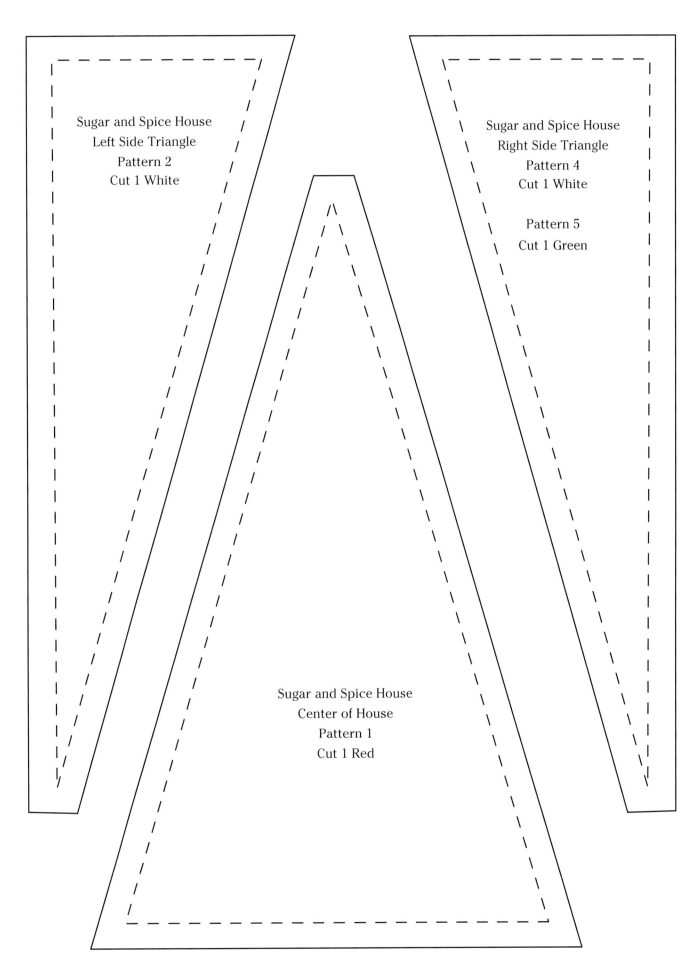

Sugar and Spice House
Left Side Triangle
Pattern 2
Cut 1 White

Sugar and Spice House
Right Side Triangle
Pattern 4
Cut 1 White

Pattern 5
Cut 1 Green

Sugar and Spice House
Center of House
Pattern 1
Cut 1 Red

Hydrangea

pieced by Judith Katz
quilted by Julie Lawson

Spring is bustin' out all over! Capture the freshness of Spring every day of the year with pretty pastels, fun plaids and favorite flower prints.

Fabulous for a newborn baby or a summer picnic, the pretty pastels in the Hydrangea Quilt invite everyone to stop and admire the flowers.

This quilt also makes a delightful summer throw for the family room or front porch swing.

instructions on pages 22 - 23

5 Blue prints

5 Green prints

5 Pink prints

5 Yellow prints

12 White prints

Hydrangea

SIZE: 46" x 54"
MATERIALS:
 E. E. Schenck Company Maywood Studio
 Hydrangea by Glenna Hailey
Purchase 1 'Sweet 16s' pack OR 32 fabrics 9" x 11"
 5 Pink prints   or ½ yd
 5 Blue prints   or ½ yd
 5 Yellow prints   or ½ yd
 5 Green prints   or ½ yd
 12 White prints   or ½ yd

Border & Binding   Purchase 1 yd Green print
Backing   Purchase 2 yds
Batting   Purchase 52" x 60"
Sewing machine, needle, thread

Fuchsia

pieced by Lanelle Herron
quilted by Julie Lawson

Too much fun! The great dimensional quality of this quilt is achieved with color placement.

You will be surprised at how easily these parallelogram shapes piece together.

instructions on
pages 24 - 25

Optional: These mixed print Fuchsia fabrics look great as Mitered borders. (See instructions for Mitered Borders on page 14).

Fuchsia Colors

SIZE: 49½" x 60½"
MATERIALS:
E. E. Schenck Company/Maywood Studio
Fuchsia by Jackie Robinson
Purchase 1 'Sweet 16s' pack OR 24 fabrics 9" x 11"
6 Cream to Tan prints	or ¼ yd each
6 Red to Fuschia	or ¼ yd each
6 Yellow to Green	or ¼ yd each
6 Lavender to Purple	or ¼ yd each

Border #1 & Binding
	Purchase 1 yd Dark Green
Border #2	Purchase 2 yds Dark Purple
Backing	Purchase 2⅛ yds
Batting	Purchase 54" x 66"

Sewing machine, needle, thread

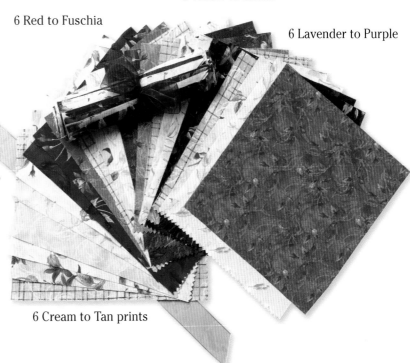

6 Yellow to Green

6 Red to Fuschia

6 Lavender to Purple

6 Cream to Tan prints

Suzanne McNeill

"I love designing with fabrics. The colors, feel and textures are exciting. Quilts are my favorite!"

Suzanne

Suzanne shares her creativity and enthusiasm in books by Design Originals. Her mission is to publish books that help others learn about the newest techniques, the best projects and popular products.

MANY THANKS to my friends for their cheerful help and wonderful ideas!

Kathy Mason
Patty Williams • Janet Long
David & Donna Thomason

Donna Kinsey for patiently editing the patterns in this book

QUILTERS
Susan Corbett   817-361-7762
Julie Lawson   817-428-5929